Autumn Wounds

Atalie Rachael

Presentation by *BookLeaf Publishing*

Web: www.bookleafpub.com

E-mail: info@bookleafpub.com

ISBN: 9789395620161

First edition 2022

DEDICATION

This book is dedicated to my closest friends and my family.

A Note Of Change

Change is a gift that saves human memory from
monotony.
And with change comes seasons.
One particular season seems to sum up all of the
seasons.
Autumn is floral hibiscus slowly turning to
shades of burgundy.
It lets us know that an end comes to good while
slowly
opening chapters of reflection in fall.
The poems that reside in Autumn also take
multiple rests in Winter and Springtime.
Because change is year round.

Beautiful Things

2

The wind makes the
fir branches move
and they flirt with me
playful as ever
Telephone poles
hang their wires
on cream white clouds
I float
in a blue dream
where time is an
emotion
and we rock
we sway
we roll
in softly tranquil
tidal wave
till nothing runs us down
but the urgency
of beating
ourselves back home
where beautiful things
reside.

Today, I Am Lugubrious

A lifetime can fit into
a long day.
There's indigo
on both sides of the
hours.
Please sweet love,
trim the gravity
from my backbone.
I'm so tired
I could weep
the sounds of my heart
into your sleeve.

"Art does not come easily
from the artist.
Sometimes we draw it from a place that is like a
dehydrated vein.
We poke at our intuition, our emotions, and our
thoughts like a desperate phlebotomist.
Do not expect us to always find the vein.
But remember us for when we do."

October

Blessing Over Burden

She said she was poetic
and she captures the loveliest
of things.
She spites the stem
that is hers
by clasping petals
and folding outwards.
She yells life
with simple statements
tucked under the garments
of her florets.
She begs kindness
unto her
and the warm
sun listens.
She is proverbial beauty
when she is least welcome.
She is Ruth
and Naomi.
And she said above all things
that she must be a blessing
and never a burden.

Daughter, Woman, Wife, & Mother.

I can carry the vagabond of August rather
fondly, if you ask me.
An old soul is meant to understand younger
things.
I can wear a long thick black sweater
with wilt white lilies embroidered on the bottom.
I can look the sky in its eye,
and see myself laughing in the creases of its
clouds.
I can take my mother on a walk someday,
and if her vision fails her, I will show her
everything so vividly
that she will hear the beauty of life in my
speech.
Like how, purple was dipped ever so slightly
into milk. And we carry our bodies of
formulated bones past
the voluptuous trees that grow them.
Lilacs.
I can marry my husband someday, and the true
ceremony
will be cast in all the years we live together.
I can protect him with fierce love and respect
him with genuine

humility. I am not always worthy of the term
"bride."
My heart nestles between the seasons,
but my veil is always his
to reveal me to him.
I can give life and home to the homeless in spirit
and carry my children upon my back. And I can see their
little fingers pointing at something in the
distance.
Just like how I'd have to explain beauty to my
mother if her
sight diminished, I'd explain beauty to my
offspring
with an eager lesson in bud at it's
back throat.
I can do it all. I know I can.
I just pray for the strength
to do it.

"Dear Extravagance.

8

You are frivolous
and silly.
You are hype
and chit chat.
You are freeway
with no journey.
You've forgotten
how to laugh
And I pity
you.
Because I learned
laughter
when I loved
and lived the moment
without worry
of attaining you.
You silly silly fool.
Thy shimmer
compares to death.
I want life.
Greenery. Held hands.
Aching ribs
from wit
that turns the soul
to giggling waters

and silly
mischief.
I'm not with apology
my dear extravagance.
Go elsewhere
for whatever it is
you mean
when you say
"follow me."
- Sincerely,
The One Not Following
You

Sun Ripened Gossip

Backyard lullabies are dandelions, in case
you didn't know.
Hummingbirds take refuge in April blossoms,
and
the sun ripens their murmuring.
Maturity is the fault for love to be wanted
with lowered voice and high strung wind.
This was how Summer
was born;
on sweetened branches
of evening
dusk.

Child's Laugh On The Beach

I hope
for a lot.
But most of all
I hope
you get tipsy
on my sunshine.
I'm not much
but I'm
at least
summertime
With a little honey
for flavor.
Sand dunes.
And lapping waves.
I am child's laugh
on the beach
And I know
it's not mature.
But I hope
for a lot.
And that
maybe I'll impact
your life a little
is hope enough.

Small Sips

Small sips of a natural thing
creates the healthiest connection.
If you force yourself to smell every
flower at once, you will not appreciate any
single one of them.
We are taught to not live a moment
at a time
because we might make friends with peace and
intimacy.
Making friends with those two variables
dissolves the idea of hurry.
If we constantly hurry, we do not reflect.
And when we do not reflect,
we do not become.

To Sit And Wait For a Ride

To sit and wait for a ride. I've been locked into the familiarity of seeking one particular car, because I call it home. To sit and wait for a ride is to wait for hope. After you get picked up, you go home, you make dinner. Then you clean the kitchen (or at least I do), and make poetry out of relaxing.

Home is simply a place to be when every other place has failed in your favor for contentment. The people you seek are the same way. Oh, to see one particular person walking into the same room you are in. To see them, memorize their monotony, and become so tuned to their every chord is the single song you walk back out the door with in the happiness that you'll come back, and hear their melody once more.

The lover cooks for you. The mother has nurturing stuck in the crook of her arm. The father, a

belt so notched with wisdom you may hallucinate your life actually beginning to make sense.

Home is where life begins. Who are we to pretend we don't need it and one another?

Darling, I beg you to go back to where you've
found a place to stay. The porch light has been
left
on just for you.

Writers Harvest

15

Type as if it were the instrument
to every inhibited breath
the thunder in your beating heart
asks you to take.
Type to say hereafter
you will leave a dance
of unbelievable
desperate things.
Type storms and irrationalities
and mature in them
like soft youth discovering
electricity in melanchious kisses.
Type,
…type.
we need the paintings,
the divinity
of freefall muse
to hold us
in our equinox.

Mona Lisa Morning

Flushed poise
barren of its night.
The birth of a universe.
She does not want to
question your ability
to see her for what she
is.
Robes of white lily
rustling against sun screens.
Beams of June
creep upon the awakened
and motion for them
to follow so far so close
into forests
of rose.

September Has Lover Eyes

17

They
look down in different colors
at the lonely.
Stars look like submarines
floating in moonflower nights
full of creatine.
The evening is embellished with time
to pass
walking through the woods
dreaming about a
past life.

FALL POEM

18

Wind
strikes a match
against chimes
And October
dances
falling leaves.
Cider and sage
melt
stale romance
where the patches
of old ghosts
cross stitch patterns
of giggling laughter
between bent
oak trees

Silent Respect - a sonnet

-

Fairest famine is that which jealousy
Compromised with disrespect for being.
Secrets make not the battle come for free.
Instead a lie is the most deceiving.
Time loosens it's waist; she knows she is short.
Best, she says to be your own cohort.
The garden needs tending, the flowers more;
Petals bruised are souls misunderstood, true.
Why the frivolous recite at my door
You who dust bowl with the darkest of hues?
Knock loudly, then prey with admiration
If you are belittled by frustration.
Never must you shame that isn't yours.
Esteem silently actions before words.

Well Off Conversation

O' wind,
blessed nocturnal breeze
I am but small
in your conversational piece
You who
so with vast a thing to say
comfort mine
discrepant tiresome way.
With soft
lips and roughened heart
I could tell you
stories of the blossom's
in dark.
Sweet wind,
have you ever seen such
an idyllic plum?
One where one wonder's
a pleasant lie
in all its saccharine melody
is from?
Dear,
this is not the inhibition
I assume life assumes
for us
For if wisdom

is held in your stride,
I'd be obliged
to finally take
some rest.

Skies Of Serenade

When the world disappoints me,
I believe in chance
per the sweet
affection of you.
I can sing.
I can do a million things.
I could fly
like the bluest bluejay
in skies of serenade
(if I so desire).
Because when you
love someone,
you can do anything.

Even Peace Is But A Thorn
(at times when you look for it)

Morning fog
and sleepless nights
intertwine their sluggish
tendrils round my arms.
My legs beg to lie
and
my body to sit.
I am a poet
in these early hours.
Toast burns
while I review instructions
for my students
English assignment.
Life is full
of instructions.
When I am not
at work,
when I am not at play,
I wish to know the commands
for peace.
Sometimes their lost
little thorns

become calluses
unyielding
to the aesthetic of a busied soul.
They preach softly
to the universe
"let me bloom
and how I will show you
my impossibilities!"

My Sister Is Character

I go for walks in the woods
and take with me the flesh
that brings all the wolves round.
My beating heart is a battle cry
silently scathing within my chest
I must bring willpower down from her
chambers
"Woman up!" she says,
And my oh me, I'm so weak.
The hills are too mighty for climbing.
But integrity is mightier
And my sister is Character, she seeks
what is right, like the powerful proverb
that leaves indents after it convicts
I the convicted
am convinced of the all knowing ways
that a woman must have
when she learns love
must be self-protective before it can
truly love again.

Autumn Wounds

When the last orchid has come to fruition,
the first thought might be about the future.
In great towns and small farms,
cottonseed is laid aside
like the burden of spirit.
Development is foliage
outlined in the background of our lives,
even beyond city lights.
There are at least twelve poems in every leaf
that falls,
and two in the palm of one hand.
Trace the skin indents till the street stops.
There is a time to bring something good to an
end.
The first full moon of Autumn
is the wound
we fill
to start over again.